What **WORD** Defines You?

By

Jeannie Brown

Acknowledgement

First and foremost, I would like to thank God, for He makes all things possible for me. He gave me the life I have and because of that, I've experienced many things that have made me stronger, wiser and more sensitive. I do my best to use all of the gifts He has bestowed upon me to help others. And, I always remain open to learning.

Secondly, I would like to thank a very special friend, who is a published writer of several fiction short stories and a novel in the works for all the time he spent reading, re-reading and editing "What Word Defines You?" His suggestions were helpful and always in the best interest of the work.

A special thank you to the following individuals for either completing the exercise themselves or for sending my request to friends, clients or students to complete and be a part of this book. Many of their words and explanations were used in the chapter entitled 'Other People's Words.' There work made it clearer and easier for others to do the exercise and to know there is no right or wrong choice. It is an individual decision.

Thank you to:

My family and friends – for taking the time needed to dig deep and arrive at their word with an explanation as to why it was chosen.

A Harper College psychology class – and the Professor who made it a class project to complete the exercise and return it to me.

Maxine of Maxine Jones & Associates – for sending my request to her client list. Thank you Melody too.

Patty, my sister – for sending my request to her colleagues.

Thank you all for your support and your belief in this book.

Table of Contents

Introduction

I am one of ten children and all of us have been married at one time or another. Similar to everyone else in the world, those of us who are married continue to work on strengthening our relationships and those of us who are single continue to search for what would make an ideal relationship.

First of all, I've discovered that the ideal relationship has flaws. In order to grow, learn and experience, there have to be differences of opinion, different perceptions and then a strong draw to making up. I wouldn't suggest looking for these differences, but I would embrace them when they arrive. This book is about a way that will help you do this.

It will help you to weed out the relationships that aren't meant to work and that will prevent you from moving forward. All of this can be accomplished before there has been too large of an investment made.

In this book you'll find questions that you may never have thought to ask a possible partner, but you'll find out soon enough, that when you do, you'll be glad you did.

It's the things we never ask that get us into trouble. Think of what is really important to you and voice it. With the exercise in this book, you'll find the path you're meant to take and if your partner is running parallel to you, or simply crossing at the intersection. Sometimes that crossing takes years to complete, but it will complete and the connection will be gone. Running side by side, each independent with a similar goal will definitely be a positive force for an ideal relationship.

What *WORD Defines You?*

Have you ever asked yourself what word defines you? What is it that keeps you going; that drives you further; that holds your interest; that fills your life and that you couldn't live without? It's not something most people think about in terms of their life existence. If you did, what word would you say defines the essence of who you are?

Before I continue, let me say, "I know there is no single word that defines any one person." Having said that, the word I'm referring to is the word that best defines the essence, the roots as it were, of who you are. From that base/root word, sprouts many other words that express who you are as well.

Which word is it that signifies the strongest of impulses, that carries your emotions and essence through trying times. This is the word I'm referring to.

Have you ever wondered how your life was compiled? Did it simply fall into place because of your upbringing, your friends, your schooling or financial issues? How often do you ask yourself what is it in life that you truly strive for? Is it as simple as getting through the day or do you have loftier hopes and dreams? And what is it inside you that has you meet or continue to strive for those hopes or dreams? With that, let's go one step further. What word best depicts what is at the root of your being?

I know we all ask ourselves what we want today or tomorrow. However the answers would only be extensions of the word that defines the essence of who we really are and what we're searching for. The stronger our desires, the more dependent we become on this word.

In the following pages, I will give examples as we move forward in my explanation. So that the fewest amount of words is used to describe something, instead of saying he/she, I will use 'he' which can stand for a man or a woman. When it is a man <u>and</u> woman, I will give them names.

Every Day Life

Every day life has all of us wanting little things to go our way daily, weekly, monthly and yearly. We may have ongoing hopes that stay with us a while or hopes that change as quickly as the temperature.

To help us understand how our word impacts our lives, I've listed a few situations here that we may have hoped for at one time or another.

Losing a few pounds; finding a parking spot close to the store; believing our significant other will remember our birthday/anniversary; knowing the insurance company will pay for Mom's medication; and that our good neighbor will return our lawn mower without our asking.

These are simply day-to-day things that would make life easier or better. If we can get to the root of why we want these things, we may find it goes much deeper than we think.

Believe it or not, there are some people who would not give any thought to any of those things. For some of us, that seems impossible because of the importance we've placed on those issues. Others may believe it's not that important or that someone else will take care of it. However, what they don't realize is that these feelings, no matter what they are, may also be connected to the word that defines them.

As an example, wanting to lose a few pounds could be a root of many different words. If your word is <u>pride</u> this would probably be a very important issue for you. You have pride in your appearance and how you carry yourself. If however, your word is <u>family</u>, the importance of losing weight may be based on the lack of energy you have and need to care for the ones you love. If your word is <u>comfort</u>, losing weight may not be an issue for you at all until it becomes a medical concern.

A second example would be the importance of a simple thing like finding a parking spot close to the store. Given the word that defines you, the reasons once again would vary. If your word is <u>fatherhood</u>, this parking spot may mean a great deal to you because it is about getting your child in and out of the store as effortlessly as possible and in the shortest amount of time. If your word is <u>challenge</u>, you may be driven to get the spot before someone else, feeling very proud that you accomplished that maneuver. If your word is <u>caring</u>, you may miss out on the spot by seconds and feel good for the person who actually got it. None of these are wrong, they are merely variations of reasoning.

In case I've mentioned your word above and you're thinking, "I wouldn't feel that way at all," I must tell you, that each of those words mean different things to different individuals. For example, perhaps an individual's word is <u>fatherhood</u>. If he has one child and misses a parking spot, but sees that a father of four successfully gets it... there may be camaraderie and he's fine with it. Also, if your word is <u>challenge</u>, it may be that this is far too small of an issue to even concern yourself with, and it doesn't become a challenge at all.

A third example would be that your significant other remembers your Birthday/Anniversary. For an individual whose word is <u>relationship</u>, this would be of enormous importance. Whereas for someone whose word is <u>structure</u>, remembering would be expected simply because it's your Birthday/Anniversary and he is your significant other. On the other hand, if your word is <u>faith</u>, you may say that if he didn't remember, it wasn't on purpose and you'd lean toward believing that he would make it up to you.

A fourth example would be the difference in feelings and action when it comes to an Insurance Company paying for your Mother's medication. There are several people who would be adamant about this. However the reasons why, would once again vary a great deal, given your word.

If your word is responsibility, this would be huge. This is what you do in life, you take on situations that need resolve and you would want to make sure that the Insurance Company was living up to their responsibilities as well. If your word is family, you'd be outraged that your Mother had to fight for something you believe she is entitled to and the connection to your mother would help you to take on the battle. If your word is growth, you may take a step back and ask yourself if, indeed, the insurance company should actually cover this medication or not and you'd read through her medical insurance to find out. Or you might find a loophole that allowed you to win, while remaining calm. If your word is caring, you may feel that it is your duty to take on your mother's expense if the insurance company doesn't pay. If your word is fun, you're not likely to be involved in this at all. It simply would never have become a thought to begin with.

The fifth and last example was your neighbor returning your lawnmower. This may seem a relatively small issue for some, while others can find it quite important. If your word is responsibility, you may feel you want it back now because your neighbor promised to return it by a certain date and didn't. It's about a promise not being kept. And that can be enormous to a responsible person. On the other hand, if your word is caring, you may never even think to ask for it back until you actually need to use it yourself. And if your word is <u>growth</u>, you may realize that this particular neighbor is not someone you will be lending things to again, while accepting the fact that he is not concerned about returning things he's borrowed.

Again, none of the above reasoning's are wrong, simply different ways of looking at a situation due to the word that defines you. However, they can come across extremely wrong to the individuals who spend their lives attempting to take care of everyone and everything. It's difficult to understand all the different ways that people think, but we must do our best.

I'm sure we've all tried to figure people out to an extent, but if we understand ourselves first, it might be easier to move on to others.

Hopefully this is becoming a little clearer to you? And, it's possible that you've known your word for some time.

However, this is not to say, that your word hasn't changed since then, due to family, lifestyle or circumstance. Later on, we'll get into how your word can change.

Back to What word Defines You. Don't let others tell you what your word is. No matter how it appears, how other people see you is a perception of theirs, but not necessarily the word you live your life by.

Let me explain…the way you live your life may be with an intent to care for others, however your style of caring may appear as bossy or condescending without you realizing it. Others may then see your word as 'control', when you say it's 'love' or 'caring'.

You shouldn't change your word, however you might take heed to what others are saying, especially if it has a negative connotation and is coming from several individuals. If your life is based around the word caring, seriously consider making adjustments to the way you show you care.

Here's another example using the word motherhood. A friend may say, "Your word is definitely motherhood." They may say this simply because you're a great mother. You can have other words show up equally as strong, and not be the base upon which you balance your life. Responsibility could have you being a wonderful mother, just as family would do the same. Using either of those two words, it's not solely about the relationship between you and your children, it's merely an extension of your word.

In this instance, know that your word is fine the way it is and accept their suggestion as a compliment. To help you know whether motherhood is your word, the following may give you guidance.

If your word is <u>motherhood</u>, I would venture to say that 80% of your attention and concentration remains with your children. The other 20% moves outside, but only to the extent that it involves your role as a mother. If your word is <u>family</u>, your husband, your children, yourself, and all of you, as a unit, holds your focus.

An example would be an outing to the park. If a woman's word is <u>motherhood</u>, her one and only focus would be on the child's needs. She wouldn't worry about what she needs as a woman or what her husband needs as a man. If a woman's word is <u>family</u>, she would find time during her child's nap to take a shower and wash her hair, then spend time with her child at the park and make sure she still had quality time to spend with her husband when he got home from work. Her focus would be split in three, not one.

Once again, if this were discussed before having children, there would be nothing wrong with any of these words and how they are perceived by each individual. However, if not, it is unfair to expect your partner to be fine with it. After all, if love and affection is what brought you together originally, then it is needed to sustain the relationship.

What we all need to know is that our perceptions of the way things should be, is just that, our perception. Everyone has their own perception and it needs to be shared with their significant other.

Some individuals will have a clear-cut reason why their word represents and defines them, as though no other word could. For them, there is no other word. Again, this is fine, but they need to understand that others have that right as well.

Some people know their word instantly. Others take a great deal of time to decipher which word it may be. Both ways are fine and again, tells us something about the individual. Take the time you need.

When I started this, I knew immediately that my word was Love. And, actually by doing the exercise I've outlined in the following chapter, I realized my word was correct. Everyone has their own description when they hear the word Love. To some it's sexual, while to others it's nurturing and still others, it's about compassion, vulnerability and acceptance.

I'm one of ten children and for me, it's always been about being there to help others. I've only recently realized that underneath I may have been hoping that others would do the same for me.

There are those of us who believe <u>love</u> is the most important thing in the world. I'm one of them. There are those who believe that being <u>responsible</u> is the most important thing in the world. Whichever word you choose, it must hold the most meaning for you in your life. It's the word that defines your essence and it's also what you are searching for. At first I didn't realize that I was searching for love. I thought I <u>was</u> love and that was good enough. If I thought that love didn't exist in other people, I don't know what I'd do. So, I believe there is good in everyone and that love exists there too. Sometimes it's hidden ever so slightly, and sometimes it appears to be buried for life. So, I not only feel the love for others, but I'm also looking for it from them.

The idea of discovering what word defines us is not to judge others on the basis of <u>our</u> word. Once we understand another's word, we can better understand the path that person walks and see how our paths coincide.

Knowing your own word helps you, but knowing the word that defines others around you can be beneficial as well. Why? Every individual has a different perception about what is normal. What you may think as radical can be quite common to another individual. This is why we have such a huge split when it comes to political and religious issues. The word that defines you is where you want your life to lead you. It is a word that holds the most important meaning in your life. See if the people in your life complement your word and you complement theirs.

Also, be sure that the word you choose is a word that can be explained to others. If you've chosen a word because others have given it to you, or because it's a word of importance to your parents, friends, etc., choose another word. Always question why you feel the way you do and go with your instincts.

I'll give you a few examples of why it would be helpful to know your own word and the word of your most intimate relationships.

A man meets a woman who is fun, exciting and loving. In her he sees everything he has ever wanted…a woman who lives in the moment. His word is <u>relationship</u>. They date for a while and discuss getting married and having a family. He pops the question and they have a fairytale wedding. In him she sees a wonderful warm and giving person. She becomes pregnant and she is brimming with excitement. He notices her focus is definitely on having this baby, which seems normal, because it is their first.

However, after the baby arrives, her focus is a tunnel that connects only to the baby. She is no longer interested in the romantic or sexual nature of the relationship and feels she has another purpose.

What happened? Can you guess what her word is? Motherhood.

Her goal in life was to have children and she has reached her goal. Now, in her mind, the only reason for intimate contact with her husband would be to have another baby. She doesn't see this as wrong, she sees it as the logical path in life for her.

Many of us have heard that women who get married and have children, change from a wife to a mother. That's definitely not true of all women. However, with some it is. Why? Because their defining word is motherhood and once they achieve that word, they may no longer have time to be wives and friends. This is extremely important for a woman who defines herself this way. However, how did the man define himself? If he defined himself as a father, then things will probably work out fine. However, if the husband defines himself as a husband or lover or his word is relationship, there are going to be problems. When your relationship to your spouse is cut off because of the birth a child, it's not fair to the spouse or to the child. The child needs to experience a healthy loving relationship between his parents as well as with his mother. And more obviously, the bridge that kept you close to your spouse has been taken away and he is left in view, but not within touch, yet still has to continue his previous promise along with added responsibility. When your choice affects another to that magnitude, something needs to be done to repair the bridge.

In this instance, the man may end up leaving, looking to fulfill his destiny, his word, relationship elsewhere.

However, if the man has chosen the word, responsible, he will probably stay true to his commitments whether circumstances change or not. Love does not need to be present and neither does happiness in order to fulfill his word. This is not to say he wants this. However, because responsibility is so prevalent in his life, he will force himself to do without. This allows the woman to reach her goal, and the man to reach his, but at what cost? If the man's word is <u>learning</u>, he can go one of two ways. He can learn to live without the attention and support of his wife or he may learn to realize that he, indeed, wants romance and love in his life and if he can't get it at home, he may leave to find it now or after the children are older.

But wouldn't it be nice, if the man who chose <u>relationship</u> had married a woman who chose <u>relationship</u> as well? Does it have to be the same word? No. <u>Relationship</u> would probably do well with <u>love</u> or <u>passion</u> or many others. However, many people are attracted to their opposite, balancing out the relationship. The thing is, knowing what your word is would help you to decide if this is something that works for you. You could discuss a whole different topic, something you hadn't thought of before.

And, keeping all this in mind, it is not to say the woman knew that <u>motherhood</u> was her word all along. Some women don't know because they never thought to ask themselves what word defines them. It may have surprised her as well.

This is also the case if a man's word is <u>success</u> and his wife's word is <u>passion</u>. The man's interest may be easily removed from the relationship due to his focus on the big house, nice car and corner office. There may not be time for the spontaneous passion that interested him before. But, until he began to attain these things, the passion he received from his wife may have been his success.

This can have the same results as the word <u>motherhood</u>. Once again the bridge that kept her close to him has been taken away and she's left in view, but not within touch. She still has to continue her previous promise to care for the children, but without the love and support and fun from her husband.

Or perhaps the man's word is <u>success</u> and the woman's word is <u>family</u>. She may be very satisfied with staying home with the kids and watching television, instead of getting dressed up and attending a formal function. She wants her family unit and he wants his success. These are things that cause issues in a marriage or any intimate relationship.

Know the word of your partner.

This all sounds very tricky, but the main thing is to be honest with yourself when selecting your word. If you're not, it can end up hurting you and your relationships.

I felt the best way to help you get started was to give you an idea of how others chose their word and why.

With this concept in mind, I started by asking my brothers and sisters what word defined them. It was very interesting. First, because I come from a large family and everyone is very competitive and I felt each person would want to have the best, if not the right, answer. However, I explained that there was no right answer, that it was an individual desire and feeling, and they each took a great deal of time to come up with their own word. I won't say which belonged to whom, but these are the answers that I got:

Love, passion, appreciation, challenge, relationships, growth, trust and faith.

Don't forget, if you choose a word as your defining word (i.e. responsible) it doesn't mean you won't be a loving person. It usually means the other person doesn't have to be, because your responsibility to them will exist whether their love stays or not. This is why you need to know what your partner's word is before you become heavily involved.

Even though having only one word sounds impossible, it's really not. Another analogy to help you understand how to choose your word could be candy. If you were told you can have only one candy bar in an aisle of thirty candy bars at the grocery store, you would no doubt choose your favorite. But that doesn't mean if you could have a different one for free, you wouldn't enjoy the second one as well. In other words, if a second one comes along with the first, great. But, if it's a choice between the two, your favorite wins out.

It's the same with your word. I look at a second word as more of a "I'd like to have my life about this" sort of choice. Whereas, your main word is exactly that, the word you live your life with. Wouldn't it be nice to be able to choose what kind of person you're interested in based on what they're really all about. Meaning, in the beginning of a relationship, many individuals try to please the other and do things they wouldn't normally do. Now, if this continues, that's fine, but if it is going to stop abruptly, it would be good to know. Knowing what changes to expect, would be helpful. Discussing your word would be a good step in the right direction.

I believe any information we receive before making the decision to commit to someone is extremely beneficial.

Here is another example of what could happen:

What about a man who defines himself as a <u>father</u> marrying a woman who defines herself as <u>passionate</u>.

The man and woman first meet and develop a very passionate relationship. We'll call them Toby and Clare. They eventually talk about getting married and having romantic getaways and possibly having a family. It sounded wonderful to both of them. However, in Clare's thirties, a promotion put her in line for a position that required a great deal of travel. She began traveling to remote places and loved the idea of meeting her husband for a passionate weekend on a romantic beach, a five-star hotel, or a hut on the Nile. Clare didn't want that to go away, so she let Toby know she was going to start taking the pill. Meanwhile, Toby saw his chance of being a father, slipping away. He had never specifically said that was his goal in life, but felt that would be the natural progression of things.

'Possibly' was the word that Clare hung onto and 'Family' was the word that Toby hung onto.

Neither Toby nor Clare are wrong, but only one of them is getting what they truly want. A discussion needs to begin.

I believe our desires partially come from how we were raised and what we've seen works or what we've seen doesn't.

Each person that I asked what their word was, took a good amount of time deciding. I thought that was wonderful that they were taking it so seriously and it helped me a great deal. It was also interesting to hear the explanation behind the word. Two or more individuals could pick the same word, but have a totally different reason for doing so. Communication is key when it comes to a relationship, at least a happy, long-lasting one.

So, my suggestion is to try this out with someone you're interested in. Be sure to tell them that there is no right or wrong answer. You may be surprised at what you find out and the number of things in a relationship that are never talked about until someone or something brings it up. Then it's a surprise and an in-depth conversation may follow. Try to stay away from arguments. No one has lied about how they felt or what they wanted, it was just never discussed.

Feelings that were originally shared are usually very real and authentic, but those feelings may not have anything to do with their word. They may feel they can keep the relationship in a different way that works for them and because you love them, it will also work for you. You may have similar feelings that show up in a completely different way. Here's an example:

A man whose word is <u>challenge</u>, sees a beautiful, intelligent woman and pursues her. Her word is <u>comfort</u>. She does not succumb to his advances for quite a while, because she is not yet sure of how she feels or if he can provide the comfort she desires. He woos her, sends her flowers and takes her out to nice places. She loves the attention and begins to relax a little with her feelings. Over a period of several months, the woman finally feels loved and comfort sets in. She opens up and lets him know how she feels about him. To her surprise, the man pulls away. What she doesn't understand is that he may be as confused as she is. The challenge is no longer there. He doesn't understand and needs it to go on. The rope that he held onto to pull her in, has disappeared. Now, she's totally there for him and him alone. For months and months he was wonderful to her in every way. Why did it change? What did she do wrong? She didn't jump in blindfolded, she made sure of her feelings before allowing love to take hold of her.

Neither of them did anything wrong.

He lives for a challenge and she was it. If her word had been <u>success</u> or <u>growth</u>, he may still feel the challenge because her focus would still not be totally on him and she would, therefore, still be a challenge. If his word had been love, he would feel wonderful when she finally accepted his love. The problem is their words did not match up. Many times, this is not discovered until after the marriage, not because either one is trying to fool the other, but because they may not have realized it themselves.

This is why when you choose your word, you choose it carefully and go with what you believe to suit you best. Then, write down the reason why. If you're honest with yourself, you will have chosen the correct word. You'll learn a lot about yourself from your own explanation.

Then you would move on to the individual you're interested in. Find out what their word is and accept what they say it is. Don't try to dismiss something you are told as fact because it's not what you want to hear. That would only hurt you in the long run. Honesty is a good thing, as long as it's delivered in a sincere and loving way.

Choosing the word that Defines You?

I'm glad you asked. The first thing you'll need is a sheet of paper and a pen. Begin by writing down all the words that have meaning to you in your life. They can be nouns, verbs or adjectives. It doesn't matter. And the number of words you have is also a personal decision. As you write them down, think about each word and what they mean to you and how they affect your life. Don't move on until you've done this.

Okay, once that's done, take a deep breath and cut the list in half. I know you're thinking, "I can't. All these words are important to me." And, I'm sure they will remain that way, but it's like food, if I asked you to list all the food you like, it would probably be a very long list too.

However, if you had to cut the list in half, I bet you could. Same idea here.

You're almost there. Now you have half the words left and I'm going to ask you to cut the list in half again. If it takes you awhile, that's okay. Because I want you to keep cutting the list in half until you are left with one word, your word, the word that you feel best describes who you are and what you could not do without.

There are no wrong answers by the way. No word is necessarily better than another, just a preference.

And something else you need to know, so you can breathe a sigh of relief. If you chose <u>strength</u>, that doesn't mean that you don't want or have love in your life. It also doesn't mean you are irresponsible. What it may mean is: <u>Strength</u> is what gets you through all the little ups and downs, the delicate situations and without that strength, you don't believe you could do it.

This applies to each and every word that is chosen.

Once again, I'll use food as my example.

Two friends and I, go to an Italian restaurant. We all decide to order baked lasagna. Noticing this, I ask both of my friends what it is about baked lasagna that they like. Friend #1 says, "It's the noodles. They are always cooked to perfection," and Friend #2 says, "no way, it's definitely the sauce... it's amazing," and they both look at me and say, "Why do you like it?" I smile and say, "For me, it's the cheese. I can't get enough of it." Shortly after, we were all eating the same thing, but experiencing it in a different way. So, if the restaurant was to change the recipe for their sauce, they may lose Friend #2's patronage. Or if they were to use a different kind of noodle, Friend #1 may venture elsewhere. The point is that the taste (i.e. importance) is placed on different things, based on what you like or where your reasoning is coming from. This is what makes you a unique individual. You don't want to be like everyone else. Because then the gift that you are will never shine through. Don't pick a word that someone else believes suits you, unless you believe it too.

Once again, remember this is <u>your</u> word, not the word others have labeled you with. A word that defines what you could not do without in your life.

After you've decided on your word, you will be asked to explain why. So, doing this exercise will give you that answer. The 'why' is what separates you from many others that may choose the exact same word.

To help you out even further, I've done the exercise myself. This way you can see how I decided on the word I did and what the reasoning was behind it. On the next page I've listed, in no particular order, the words that fill my life. Following that, I've cut the list in half and explained why I took out each word that I did.

Once again, I've used reasoning based on where I'm coming from. It is neither the correct nor incorrect way to choose. It is simply meant to be an aid or path to choosing your own individual word.

I cannot emphasize enough how important it is that you make your own decision. You know yourself better than anyone else, even if you think you don't. You will however need to take the time to listen to what it is that touches your heart or gets your pulse racing. If it's a word that scares you, it's probably the right word. But, now you get to give this word a description that defines you. It may very well mean something entirely different than the meaning given in the dictionary or by a close friend.

Be honest with yourself. If you're not, there is no point in doing the exercise.

Okay! I think you're ready now. The next page will walk you through how to begin to understand yourself in a way you never thought you needed to.

This is how I started:

Love

Caring

Friendship

Activity

Fun

Strength

Challenge

God

Relationship

Writing

Passion

Understanding

Giving

Connection

Success

Spiritual

Healer

Happiness

Conversation

Okay, now I've cut my list in half:

Love

Friendship

Fun

God

Relationship

Passion

Giving

Spiritual

Healer

Happiness

And, now I'll explain why I took out the words that I did.

I took out ~~Caring~~, because Love of everyone, Friendship and Relationship would encompass caring for me.

I took out ~~activity~~, because for me, loving, caring, understanding and connecting are activities that I enjoy very much.

I took out ~~Strength,~~ because my strength comes from God and Love and a connection with others.

I took out ~~Challenge,~~ because living through Love is challenge enough.

I took out ~~Writing~~ because although I love to write, if I had writing, but no love or friendships in my life, or no spiritual connection, I'd have nothing to write about.

I took out ~~Understanding,~~ because Love, Relationship and Friendship encompass Understanding for me.

I took out ~~Connection,~~ because Friendship and Relationship are the result of connecting with someone in a loving way.

I took out ~~Success~~, because if I have Love, I am successful.

And finally, I took out ~~Conversation~~, because being with someone can mean more than words could ever say. And many of my conversations are my silent prayers to God.

As I mentioned before, the words I've taken out, will still live within me. I've not given up on strength, understanding or caring. I simply feel I can have what I need, in the words I still have left.

Now I've cut my list in half again, and I've shown another way of connecting the words I've let go, to the words that remain. I don't want to give you too much.

I want you to think and decide for yourself why you choose the words you do.

Words I've Kept	Words I Let Go
Love	(<u>God</u> is Love)
Relationship	(<u>Friendship</u> is created through Relationship)
Passion	(<u>Giving</u> is my passion)
Spiritual	(The <u>Healer</u> lives within my Spiritual self)
Happiness	(<u>Fun</u> in one's life, brings happiness)

Five words left, cut in half again are:

Love

Relationship

Passion

Whew! Okay, now for my word. It's easy with only three words left.

What word defines me is *Love.*

<u>Love</u> connects me to God and to every living thing in the universe. And I don't have to be physically with someone to sense that love. Through love, I feel connected

to the trees, the flowers and the animals as well. Love is what I strive to feel coming from and going to all living things on a daily basis.

And of course, all of the words I originally chose will continue to be a part of who I am as well, but the one word I would not want to do without is Love.

Now, why don't you give it a try.

In the next chapter, I've listed some of the words chosen by others. I've listed them in one column and in the middle column I've listed the definitions found in the Microsoft Word dictionary. Then, in the third column I've written down the meaning this word has for me. Please feel free to jot down your own definition of each word as well. Or you may circle a definition already there. This will help you to become more familiar with what words mean to you. And, as we all know, our words create our reality. So, it's important that you are using the word that works for you.

Identifying the words and Definition

WORD	Dictionary Defintion	My Definition
Love	Feel affection for Adore Worship Be in love with Be devoted to Care for Find irresistible Be keen on	*Care for Everyone*
Passion	Fervor Obsession Infatuation Excitement Enthusiasm Zeal Craze	*Intense Desire*
Appreciation	Approval Admiration Positive Reception Enjoyment Pleasure Thanks Gratitude	***Aknowledgement***

WORD	Dictionary Defintion	My Definition
Challenge	Confront Defy Face Brave Face up to Dare Dispute	*To question/To Grow*
Friendship	Companionship Amity Acquaintance Camaraderie Closeness Familiarity Alliance	*Enjoy a closeness*
Growth	Enlargement Increase Expansion Development Augmentation Intensification Escalation	*Open to Change*
Faith	Confidence Reliance Trust Conviction Belief Devotion Loyalty	*Trust in God and His Love*

WORD	Dictionary Defintion	My Definition
Relationship	Association Connection Affiliation Rapport Bond Liaison	*Love and Trust*
Giving	Charitable Philanthropic Generous Open handed Benevolent Bountiful	*Sharing*
Spiritual	Religious Saintly Pious Sacred Devout	*Belief inGod/Spirit/ Love/Me*
Heal (er)	Cure Mend Make well Restore to health	*One who heals all* through Love
Happiness	Contentment Pleasure Cheerfulness Joy Glee Bliss	A *very good place within*

WORD	Dictionary Defintion	My Definition
Fun	Amusing Enjoyable Entertaining Pleasurable Enjoyment Excitement Cool	*Makes me laugh*
Status Quo	existing state of affairs general state of things keep things as they presently are No change	*Same*
Righteous	Morally Upright Without guilt or sin Morally justifiable Good, Honest Right-minded	*Standing for what's right*
Catalyst	Channel Medium Mechanism Method Vehicle	*Someone who gets things moving*
Optimism	Hopefulness Cheerfulness Confidence Sanguinity Buoyancy	*Glass is always ½ full*

WORD	Dictionary Defintion	My Definition
God	Deity	*Love & Life*
	Spirit	
	Divinity	
	Supernatural Being	

Other Peoples Words

Following, are responses I received from friends, family and psychology students.

The statements stand by themselves, as I received them, without the name of the individual who wrote them. They were usually received as an email. In each statement I have bolded and highlighted the word they chose.

The reason I have included them is to help you to see how different everyone is, yet, at the same time, how wonderful. Everyone has a reason for how they feel, what they do and what they say.

You will see that two people may have chosen the same word, but the description of their word may differ quite a bit.

Hopefully after reading these, it will help you to be honest with yourself and you will choose a word that is truly right for you. Here are the words that Define them:

What *WORD* Defines You?

**Love** is my (author's) word. For me it's about feeling the emotions of people, the desires and the gratitude, the frustration and the sadness. All of which come from the love or lack of love that lives within them. Love is what guides me, motivates me and has me take the extra time for people in general or someone very special. When something wonderful happens, it's my heart that cries with happiness. And anything that comes from my heart is cloaked in love. I want everyone to feel that love for others; to want to reach out and make a difference whenever they can; to feel that love come back to them tenfold. For me this is my strength, my passion, my life.

What *WORD* Defines You?

*A word from a good Friend...*My word is **_Learning_**.
I believe that I'm here to become the best person I possibly
can. To do this, I have to learn about myself, the world
around me, and the unseen, but certainly sensed
connections, that I (we) have to the universe, the world and
our souls. Learning is a never ending quest. I want to learn
to write like F. Scott Fitzgerald, to feel with the intensity of
a jazz musician and to love like Jeannie.

What *WORD* Defines You?

My word would be **_Spirituality_**. I don't mean
religious-ness, or woo-woo new-Age floatiness. It's not
something I cling to or hide behind. It's not something that
hands me a dogma I live by and don't question. I just mean
the certainty that more is going on here than a collection of

physical things. If I thought reality (whatever that is) was limited to what is available to my physical senses, I can't imagine how I would cope. If you have a better word for it, I'm open.

What *Word* Defines You?

Okay, you asked. My word is ___challenge.___

Challenge has made me who I am throughout life--- in high school I was the only girl in my calculus class and ended up being the only A---at birth I had a turned foot and was not put into athletics to avoid disappointment, but I broke records at my grade school in several athletic events.

What *Word* Defines You?

__Compassionate__ - I have a very caring and giving heart. I have a desire to help out those in need. I have spent a good portion of my life helping others out or putting others needs before my own because I know what it is like to struggle and need a helping hand. My heart is very open and I have always felt that I need to do what I can to help out or make a difference to others in a big or small way.

What *WORD* Defines You?

My word slash words are **being _me_.** I'm amazed and awwhhed by who I am and the choices I make more now than ever. The opportunity to be me, not someone else's definition of who I could or should be is freeing and feeds my curious and co creative spirit. I find my greatest frontier lies within my control and within my reach but the potential is unbounded. So for sure the word is **ME**.

What *WORD* Defines You?

<u>**Fun**</u> - Having fun is everything I look for in life. Having fun makes me happy. I try to make everything I do

in life fun. I would give up everything in my life to have fun forever. Having fun means I'm living and that's all I care about.

What *WORD* Defines You?

Growth – A day without some type of growth is a wasted day.

What *WORD* Defines You?

My word is **appreciation** because in your terms it is the energy that I seem to require most from others in order to fill me up. I am a doer therefore I do not need others to do for me. I like to do for others that I involve myself with and mostly I only really long for genuine appreciation from them. This even applies to things in my life like sports. Some might think of it as the wanting of adoration or praise but I believe for me that I just want to be appreciated by my teammates because I did the best I could and aided in their cause. Even growing up, I played only team sports and not individual sports where I would be singled out and praised more if that is what I desired. I was pressed by my brothers to be the best and sought only their appreciation for how I played. I always found it interesting how some guys could rattle off dates and years of big games or championships won and the score and I could not. I used to think that maybe I did not care as much as they did, but I guess maybe these just weren't the things about playing that were important to me. I could go on with the aspects of my life, but I think you get the gist.

What *WORD* Defines You?

Determination: I feel this brings out the "fighter" in all of us. It is part of your inner strength that gets you through whatever you are going through in life, good or bad. When there's something we want or want to do and want it bad enough, our determination kicks in and makes us get it. As long as you are determined to overcome whatever you feel is holding you back or what you are trying to reach in your life you will succeed. I think if we didn't have determination in us we wouldn't really get anywhere.

What *WORD* Defines You?

My word is **_Relationships_** why? They are what fills my life- with happiness and sadness and everything in between. My relationships with people have allowed me to live out all the different sides of me. They have brought me so much joy and laughter and have answered so many questions over the years. Whether it be Kevin or the boys, Mom, a sister, a brother, a niece, a nephew an in-law. a best friend, a close friend, a good friend or a new friend. Every one of these relationships have brought more meaning to my life than I would have ever known without them and have changed me in ways that I'll never truly realize. So these are the reasons this is my word. Thanks for asking!!!

What *Word* Defines You?

Faith – There are so many ups and downs, problems, etc. in life. If I didn't believe that God was watching me and taking care of me like He has, I don't know what I'd do. There have been so many times in my life, I've been desperate and had no way out and suddenly He took care of it. It makes it a lot more natural and easier to have an optimistic outlook.

What *Word* Defines You?

Motherhood - Becoming a mother was the best thing I've ever done. Once I did, I knew it was what life was all about for me. Nothing else has ever been as important and fulfilling. My life would be empty without my children.

What *WORD* Defines You?

Catalyst - I tend to start new things for myself. Indulging in new opportunities constantly. I invoke change upon those around me. I would feel very dissatisfied with a stagnant life. Good or bad, I enjoy and learn something from every new experience.

What *WORD* Defines You?

Loyal - Is important to me, because I feel it's very important that people who I care about can depend on me do to the right thing by them no matter how difficult.

What *WORD* Defines You?

Fatherhood - Following in my father's footsteps and being there for my kids, is what is the most intuitive for me. Everything else is a part of life and wonderful, but being a father is everything.

What *WORD* Defines You?

<u>Smiles</u> - are a sign of happiness, optimism, good relationship, positive thoughts, openness to share, and the first sign of a good character. I always prefer meeting someone who has a smile versus a grimace on their face. My life contains lots of great inner smiles too, including for my two great sons, wonderful family & friends, good health, and when meeting someone new who greets me with a smile on their face!

What *WORD* Defines You?

<u>Trust</u> - I believe that there are many words that make up who I am, but one of the prominent ones is trust.

I have found that my nature is to trust people until they prove to me I shouldn't - which in some instances takes a very long time.

What *WORD* Defines You?

Respect - I chose this word because I believe without respect in my heart I'd be a very miserable unhappy person. If you don't respect yourself, no one else will. How can you love someone if you don't respect them. How can you professionally perform well if you don't respect the job and business choices you make. If you didn't respect the differences of opinions and life choices others make you'd have no friends, spouse, significant other, or happy children.

What *WORD* Defines You?

I think I am going to go with *righteous* in trying to do right .... " from my perspective.

I realize the word association is not always a positive perspective as everyone is entitled to their own opinion of what is right(eous).......

Yet I am pretty sure this direction is one that I have lived by for a long time with only an occasional diversion from its path ...

What *WORD* Defines You?

Love is the word that defines the essence of what my family is to me and what I could not live without.

What *WORD* Defines You?

Relationship – because this word encompasses it all. It includes friendship, my husband, my children and family all into one.

What *WORD* Defines You?

I guess if I must use only one word it would be **_family_**. My family is so so important to me. When I grew up, my immediate family (mother, father, brothers, sisters) was broken. I suffered for it. I was determined to have an intact, close family – and I do. It means everything to em, and I constantly hear from my kids and step kids, how much our family means to them.

What *WORD* Defines You?

Status-Quo would be my word. Why? Because I don't like change. I like things and people in my life close to me to stay the same. I can't imagine my life without the feeling of status quo.

What *WORD* Defines You?

I would have to say *Passionate!* Passion is the foundation of Inspiration. If I am Passionate about a cause, activity or project, Inspiration follows and what would usually be called work is no longer work. It becomes play. With no Passion, life itself becomes work and boring.

What *WORD* Defines You?

I guess mine would be **_Christian_**. Before I found Jesus I was a lost soul. But now that Jesus saved me, he saved me from so many things. This is the path I had to take to have a personal relationship with the living god. As a result, I have a much better life and more of a heart for people.

What *WORD* Defines You?

Acceptance is my word. But it isn't about my being accepted by others. Acceptance is about me accepting people as they are, where they are. It is about being totally non-judging of anything or anybody. I try very hard to live up to that lofty standard…failing more than I succeed.

What *WORD* Defines You?

Friends - Because when you are truly friends you have great communications and care about each other's feelings, whether in good times, bad times and in sickness.

What *WORD* Defines You?

Perfectionist - I am almost always fearing failure. It took me a long time to even come up with this word. I realize it is impossible to be perfect but that doesn't stop me from trying. No matter what I do, it is never good enough for me. What is perfect anyways? For me, it is subjective. This word is important to my life because it mostly affects me negatively. The drive to be perfect affects all aspects of my life.

What *WORD* Defines You?

Faith is the most important thing to me. Without it, I could be as negative as the next person. So, you can either use the word faith, faithful, believer, or accepting.

What *WORD* Defines You?

Connection - is the opposite of ostracism. It is the link between things. It is being a part of everything, which we are. In dance it is the tool of communication. In communication it is a feeling of togetherness. I enjoy connection in life as I enjoy touching and being touched.

It would be less without it. I believe it is a big part of why we bother with these human bodies.

What *WORD* Defines You?

My word would have to be **_Appreciation_**. For me it is two-sided, one side being the appreciation for others;

their skills, courage, honesty, vulnerability, strength, creativity, boldness, power and their human-ness.

On the other side it would be receiving appreciation for the littlest of actions or words, the smallest of offerings or assistance, to a larger commitment of help, support, love, friendship and strength.

Being appreciated validates me by saying I'm recognized as a caring and loving person that feels deeply about how others are treated.

I live by "Do unto others as you'd have them do unto you". I believe we all have something, or things special to offer this world and those gifts should be recognized, brought out and embraced, about and for that person, so we can all share in the gifts that God gave us.

What *Word* Defines You?

The word that best defines me is _**stressless**_. This word defines me because I really don't ask for much from other people and out of life. I just want to do what I want to do with no stress or hassle, often compromising things that other people may find important like success, money & power to get that feeling of peacefulness and relaxation. This word also accentuates some of the more important things to me that would cause stress if they went awry: health, relationships, family & love.

What *WORD* Defines You?

Perseverance - Life throws all sorts of obstacles and distractions in your way, without the ability to focus on the end result, I would not be able to do some of the things that I hope /get to do. It crosses over for people/ relationships/tasks as well. Without the ability to move through it and not get bogged down by the smaller things, the overall result would not be possible. All of the tasks and problems are there for a reason and serve to teach and focus the energy onto your goal, and ultimately make it possible to reach the goals that you set for yourself.

What *WORD* Defines You?

Adventurous - I am always seeking out new things to try, new places to visit, new cultures to experience. I love to travel and see every new experience as an adventure. My pursuit of adventure keeps me energized and full of positive energy. This word describes me because I could not imagine living my life without it.

What *WORD* Defines You?

Seeker - I am always searching for wisdom, purpose, hope, looking to be better, stronger, smarter, wondering about why I'm here and though I think I know, I continue to search for validity and the ultimate confirmation of meaning.

What *WORD* Defines You?

Resourceful - I believe in taking a little and make it go a long way. This has been my better attribute in life. Keeping it simple sometimes is all you really need to solve big problems.

What *WORD* Defines You?

Happiness - As long as I'm happy, my life is good. That's what I strive for is just to be happy. That's why I work and go to school, so in the future I can make sure (to my best abilities) that I'm happy.

What *WORD* Defines You?

Faithful - In so many ways it is expressed in my life. I am a faithful friend. I am faithful to my family obligations. My spiritual faith is the most important thing in my life. It is what gives my life meaning and purpose.

What *WORD* Defines You?

<u>*God*</u> - God put me here on this earth, so I wouldn't be here without him. My life is his to do what he pleases with. It's dedicated to him. Every breath I breathe, every step I walk, I do in his name. I can't imagine my life without him because I'd be completely lost and living in darkness.

What *WORD* Defines You?

<u>*Optimistic*</u> - Staying positive is very important in my life because once you get down on yourself, everything else seems to get worse. Always keep your head high and things will turn around for the better. You can't look at life as half empty, look at it as half full. You always have to look at things that are on the brighter side because there are people out there that always have it worse than you.

What *WORD* Defines You?

Persevere - This word pretty much defines how I've lived and continue to live my life, along with the way the rest of my family has and continues to live theirs. As I was a child, our family persevered through difficult times with 2 hard-working and loving parents trying to take care of 4 kids. As a young woman and single mother, my daughter and I persevered through many hardships. As my daughter grows, she perseveres through the results of some bad decisions she has made in her life. As my parents age, they continue to persevere through hard times as they continue to work to pay bills. I truly believe that no matter what difficulties arise, there is always a way to solve them and there is always something to learn and appreciate, no matter how hard things can get. There is always a way.

What *WORD* Defines You?

Relationships - Without my relationship to God and to other people, life would be lonely and very meaningless.

What *WORD* Defines You?

Sacrifice - I chose this word because all my life either in my personal or professional life I've had to sacrifice something. It's all about looking at it like it's not what you're losing, rather what you are gaining from that sacrifice.

Your word in the Business World

Knowing the word that defines you, not only helps you in your personal life, but also in the business world. One of the reasons for this is because you don't want to accept a job that on the surface seems to fit what you want at the moment, only to find out a couple months down the road, that it's not at all what you had in mind. How can you avoid that? Well, once you've figured out what your word is, see how it relates to what brings you closer to that word, day to day.

You may very well have the skills for the position, but if it's not feeding your word on a regular basis, you won't be happy.

Here's an example:

You, as a woman accept a position as a Networking Analyst for a 500+ attorney firm. You're required to carry a beeper. Your word is <u>diversity</u>.

Your explanation of <u>diversity</u> is: "because I enjoy change. I like things different all the time. I don't like being stuck doing the same thing every day, all day long."

Later it's found out that you are a member of an Improv Troop that performs three nights a week and you will not be able to answer your beeper during those shows. As you can see, you may not be the best fit for this position.

Can you do the job if you're available? I'm sure you can. But, if you're not available, it really doesn't matter.

On the other hand, if you as a woman accept the same position and your word is also <u>diversity</u> but your description of the word is "dealing with different people in life, is what it's all about. Having the opportunity to answer different questions, come up with different suggestions and work with different people on many levels is something I enjoy."

Obviously, the second example's description of your word, would fit the position better.

Originally, you may have looked at it like this: One woman likes her job and the other doesn't want to put the time in. But, there is so much more to it, than that. The reason behind it, is what will help you to make the correct choices in the future.

When you are doing something you love, your passion is heightened, your stamina is lengthened and more endorphins will be released within your brain to relieve pain, stress and bring happiness. Therefore, you need to take the time to figure out how your word relates to your future, to have that happen.

Granted, there will be jobs you take, simply because you need the money and you have no expectation of getting anything out of it, other than a paycheck. However, if you are truly looking for a career or a part time job to keep busy...take the time to see where you could be the happiest. And you can, if you figure out what word defines you first.

Here's an example of how different your word becomes, given your own explanation of it.

Let's take two men whose word is <u>success</u> and see how the description each has given their word changes the word itself. We'll call man #1, Jim, and man #2, Roland. Jim may say that success means finding his niche in life and allowing himself to be happy there; whereas Roland may say that success to him would mean holding a very highly regarded position in a Fortune 500 Company. Having people report to him, would have Roland feeling successful. However, Jim feels successful if he does what he truly loves and gets paid enough to make ends meet. Same word, but completely different goals.

If each of them had a friend that knew they were looking for work, but all they knew is that their friend wanted to be successful, it would depend on the friend's definition of successful, that would determine the type of job he might find for his friend.

Suppose your word is <u>challenge</u> and nothing excites you more than proving you can get any position you apply for. You go for a position, get it, but soon after become unenthused with the work.

Or, having your word be challenge, you get the position and become even more enthused about the job as you delve into it.

This is why it's so important to have the reason behind the word that defines us.

I'm guessing the first reason for choosing <u>challenge</u> could be because you love short-term challenges or challenges you can quickly surpass. Once the challenge is met, the excitement is gone. While the second reason you may have chosen the word <u>challenge</u> is because life is a challenge and you look at more long term goals, so anything you take on, you are bent on meeting the challenge no matter how long it takes. It's the same word with a totally different agenda behind it. It would be nice to know which one applies to you.

Party Game

Here's a fun way to find out how to get to know people a lot better than you thought possible. This game can be played in a personal setting or a professional setting. Throw a "What Word Defines You" party.

The title alone will have people wondering what it's all about. When they ask, tell them it's simply a get-to-know-you party. Have the usual pizza and soft drinks or beer, so everyone is relaxed. Encourage everyone to mingle before the game begins. Let them know that the more they know about the others, the better chance their team will have of winning.

After about 30 minutes, you can introduce the game. "What Word Defines You?" is a game, that as you may have guessed, is about the Word that defines each of us. This is how it works. You will have everyone count off, one, two, one, two, etc., until no one is left. All of the one's will step to one side of the room and all of the two's to the other.

Let's say there are twenty people. So, we should have ten people on one side of the room and ten people on the other side. Now, have each team pair up within their group. Pick a person they think they may know better than the others. If there is an odd number, put three people together. Okay! There should be enough chairs set up for everyone and the chairs should be at least three feet apart. Everyone take a seat, one seat away from your partner. Hand out 5x7 pads of paper or 5x7 pieces of paper with a clipboard. Have each individual write their name on the top left side of the paper, and just below that, ten words that mean a great deal to them. They can be nouns, adverbs, adjectives, it doesn't matter. Words that describe a portion of their life.

When you suggest to proceed, have anyone not done, raise their hands. When they've finished, have them write down the reason for each word, directly across from it. It should explain the importance of this word in their life. Give them a little longer for this part of the game. No one is allowed to share any of this information with anyone else yet.

Be sure to let them know that there are no right or wrong answers. This is simply a 'get to know you' game.

Again, check by a show of hands to be sure they are finished. Then, tell them to cross out five of their words, leaving their favorite five.

After everyone is finished choosing their favorite five, tell them to cross out all but one. Explain that this one word is the basis or root for where all of the other words come from. The other words are still a part of their lives, but this one word is the one they could not live their life without.

Once that's done, have them fold the paper up so no one can see it and put it in their pocket.

Okay! The first pair from Group One and Group Two needs to come to the front of the room. Starting with Group One, the first pair, taking turns, will ask their partner What Word Defines Me? The partner has two chances to get it right. If they get it right, have the individual take the paper out of their pocket and show the host. Their team will get ten points and the individual will explain why that is the Word that Defines Them. If they do not get it right, then the pair standing from Group Two gets one chance to guess what Word Defines the person from Group One. If they get it right, they get fifteen points. If no one gets it right, the individual will get an Index Card with a large ? on it.

Then the partner who did the guessing, will now ask his/her partner What Word Defines Me? And the same rules apply.

After the first pair of Group One is finished, then the first pair of Group Two has their turn and Group One remains at the front until they are finished. Then both pairs will sit down and the second pair from each group will come to the front. This will continue until all the pairs from each group are completed.

After all pairs are completed, anyone with an index card with a large red ? on it, will come to the front.

Group One and Group Two will designate one individual in their group to ask two questions to help them determine this individual's word. (i.e. Is work important to you? or Is family important to you? etc.) The word you think is theirs may not be used in the questions or the answers, at least not the words you are going to choose as their word. (i.e. Is <u>love</u> important to you? Is <u>success</u> important to you?) If you asked these questions, you would not be able to choose <u>love</u> or <u>success</u> as the individuals' word. After the four questions have been answered, both groups will write down on a sheet of paper what they believe his/her word is. Twenty points will be given for this, if it's correct. If both groups are correct, both groups get the points.

Add up the points and see how well each team did. An awareness prize of some sort (or gift certificates) can be given, if you like.

If anyone has questions for their teammates or the individuals on the other team, this would be a good time to ask them. You may want to know why people chose a certain word for you. What made them think it would be yours? You'll be surprised at how much you'll have learned about yourself and about the others around you.

Sometimes the biggest surprise is realizing what word other people think is yours. It gives you insight as to how your actions manifest themselves and how others perceive you.

Remember, the key is to make it 'fun,' not serious. You'll end up having a great time and learning a lot about each other in the meantime.

People will probably continue to talk about their words with everyone afterward, which is the point of the game.

You'll know what people you connect with and what ones you don't.

Can Words Change?

Most definitely. Words can change and meanings can change, just as your life changes. But only we, ourselves, know which words may never change or at least how deeply embedded these words and meanings are to us.

I guess what you need to do is ask yourself why you chose the word you did and why you want to change it. What word would you like in its place? You can start by writing down the word you originally chose and write down the reasons that it no longer works for you. Do you feel this word let you down? Do you feel it wasn't strong enough or supportive enough to your purpose in life? On paper, change it to a new and improved word. Now write down why you chose this new word and what it holds for you that the first word didn't'.

You may find out that all you need to do is adjust the meaning of the original word to better suit you now.

Also, be sure you are not changing your word for someone else. It may work for a short period of time, but usually not for the long haul. Your word is about who you are and that is not something someone else can change. That's why it helps to know in the beginning what word defines the individuals who have the potential to play a major role in your life. Relationships are a lot like stocks. Once you've invested your heart and your time (your money), you begin to feel the hit would be too enormous to pull out and re-invest somewhere else. So many times we stay where we shouldn't. But if you talk it out (plan it out) in the beginning, your investment, is something that hasn't been decided yet and can be moved without too much pain (penalty).

Acknowledge who you are and what works for you, before you try to acknowledge what works for others.

Compatible or not?

That's a hard question to answer in a broad sense. You would need to take the first word along with its individual meaning and put it side by side with the second word and its individual meaning. Then you can begin. You can't take the word <u>passion</u> and put it along side <u>challenge</u> and know if it works out or not without knowing the meaning of each word for the specific individual who owns it.

I hope this makes sense to you. In other words, the word itself is not necessarily what owns the meaning, it's you who owns it. At least that's the only meaning that counts. It is a perception of meaning for you. It may have come about because of how you were raised or because of the friends in your life or it may have started long before that.

Here's an example: If for instance, my word is <u>sharing</u>, it may not mean sharing in the sense that you think of sharing. It could mean that I can't imagine living in a world where people didn't share with me. Or it could mean that I can't imagine living in a world where people didn't share their innermost feelings. Or it could mean I can't imagine living in a world where people didn't share things with each other.

Once again, all of these meanings are fine. None are right or wrong, they are simply the definition you have given the word. And to know this definition, would be helpful to the people around you.

Another example is <u>love</u>. This is my word, but if I hadn't told you in a previous chapter what love means to me, you wouldn't know. For example, it could mean that I can't imagine a world where people didn't love me. Or it could mean that I can't imagine a world where I couldn't have an intimate love to share my passion with. For me, it means I can't imagine a world where love and caring for others didn't exist. So you see there is a big difference and until you get to the explanatory level, you wouldn't be able to match with another word successfully.

Another example is how someone shows love. One parent might show love to his children by disciplining them and pushing them to be better. Another, by reading to his children, hugging them and telling them how much he loves them. A third may feel that leaving them alone to learn the ups and downs of life on their own, is true love. Some parents believe they should do everything they can for your child, whereas others believe children should be taught to work for what they want, to appreciate their accomplishments. So you see, it's not the word itself that explains the individual, it is the meaning of the word to the individual who chose it. Knowing this meaning, this perception, is what will help people to understand one another much better and to understand themselves as well.

Think of all the different examples of people there are in the world. How many times have you looked at someone and thought, "why in the world would he/she do that?" And you truly have no idea. And the reason for that, is because you may have heard them say how much they love their family, but then hear them say 'no' to what you would consider a simple request. Using your description of the word "Love," you may have said 'yes' in a heartbeat

Okay! Let's move on and say that we have now reached this level with the word <u>passion</u> and <u>success</u>. For this individual, the word <u>passion</u> means an obsession. It still sounds a bit non-specific. So asked further, we find it is an obsession for cooking, cleaning and entertaining. The second individual's meaning for success is moving up in the corporate world.

Okay so let's call success Bill and passion, Cindy. Bill is out making the most of his skills and moving up the corporate ladder. He works late on many occasions and at a moment's notice invites a client or his boss to dinner. Cindy is at home making sure that their home could be the centerfold for Home & Garden Magazine and baking a homemade apple pie from apples she picked herself. This could be a very good match. Bill does not have enough time at home to make a mess or interfere with Cindy's home making and Cindy has all the time she needs to obsess about the order of her home and is thrilled when Bill brings clients home for dinner.

Bill looks good in the bosses/clients' eyes and Cindy is thrilled to share her home and her cooking with them.

They may also share a very good personal relationship, due to the fact that both are having their words (goals) met.

Now if Cindy's definition of <u>passion</u> was different and it meant intense desire for love in the physical sense and Bill's definition of <u>success,</u> was still the same and Bill worked late nights on a regular basis, Cindy might not understand.

Cindy would ultimately be sitting home nights looking at her watch, wondering why he wasn't home yet. When he arrived home, he would probably not receive a friendly greeting, at least not after it had happened more than a few times. If Bill called with less than a few hours notice and Cindy had to prepare a meal for four, she may be less than enthused.

These are always issues that are never discussed because no one thought to. Bill and Cindy may have talked about how much they loved each other and when he was feeling down, Cindy may have said that she would be there to support him and when Cindy wanted his attention in the beginning, Bill was probably more than available to her.

Neither one explained exactly what they meant. Bill may have taken her words as a promise that whatever he needed to do to make it, she would understand and support him. But, how could she make that promise, not knowing what that would entail?

She may have felt that because he said, "I could make love to you every day and all night long for the rest of my life" in the midst of passion, that he meant it literally. This is not anyone's fault, but it does put them in a bit of a situation.

Passion is a wonderful word and a great many people use it. However, like all of the other words, it can pull us in many directions.

Many men may say their word is passionate. But, what exactly does that mean? If you ask about what, you may hear the following. I'm passionate about football; about basketball; about baseball; about hockey. And they aren't lying; they are truly passionate about it. It's probably not the passion most women are hoping for, unless of course they are equally passionate about sports themselves. My point is: saying "My word is passionate," doesn't explain a lot without specifics to back it up.

Some people will say they are passionate about anything that interests them. A follow-up question would be: Do you see your interests changing quite frequently or once you find something to be passionate about, have you found a place to remain? If the answer is, "it depends…if someone introduces me to something exciting and I think I would be interested, I could very easily become passionate about it."

This person needs to sit down and re-evaluate what his word really is. He may be a passionate person, but what I would get from the statement above is that his word is more likely to be something like Excitement.

Or I would say that his definition of Passion is a never ending passion for life, meaning he likes change.

Find out, not only the word of an individual you may be interested in, but also the meaning this individual has given his word. It will give you a lot to talk about and trust me, it will be an interesting conversation.

Two people who have a focus on something other than each other or another individual, may have the potential for a wonderful relationship, if, of course, they are living their word. If they aren't and want the partner to be there for them, it would be dependent on what their partner's word and meaning is.

The main thing is to ask the simple question…What word Defines You? And Why? You'll learn a great deal about yourself and others. And the more information you find out about yourself, the more information you'll be able receive from others. For instance, you can't be expected to understand someone else's behavior, if you don't know why they're behaving the way they are. And many times these individuals don't yet understand their own behavior either.

Another example might be the words "Status quo" and "Growth." First, find out the meaning behind each word. In this instance, "Status quo" means to dislike change of any kind in the relationship and/or family. The word "Growth" for this example means a constant yearning for new and exciting things.

Let's call "Status quo", Chris and "Growth" will be Joshua. What does the present looks like for Chris? To know if there's change, you need to know what exists now. One scenario would be they both work, come home, have dinner, watch TV and go to bed, only to get up and begin again. A second scenario could be that they are always trying new and exciting things.

That's a big difference. That's why it's so important to ask these questions. Don't assume anything about your spouse, your friend or your business partner. If you want a relationship that works, stop and ask the individual their word and what it means.

If Chris has the first scenario, this relationship will hit a snag. However, if the second scenario fits Chris, it may be something that fulfills Joshua's need for growth as well.

In all examples a male or female can take the role. And just to prove this, the following example will have a man and a woman taking on both the first and second word.

Beth and Sam and David and Sara are two couples that have chosen the exact same words, <u>comfort</u> and <u>relationship</u>.

For Beth and Sam, these words work. Here's why: Beth chose the word <u>comfort</u> and she defines her word as follows: "When I feel I am truly loved and cared for, I too can be more loving and giving because I'm no longer afraid to truly express myself. I then feel <u>comfort</u> in my relationship."

Sam chose the word <u>relationship</u> and defines his word as follows: "I cannot imagine being with someone that I don't have a personal and intimate connection with and who feels the same about me."

They are both on separate paths leading to the same goal. There will be friendship, growth and love which will give Sam his <u>relationship</u> and Beth her <u>comfort.</u>

For David and Sara, these words do not work and here's why:

David chose the word comfort. He defines his word as follows: "I want to be able to come home from work, have a beer and watch the game. If I get a belly, it shouldn't matter. She should love me for who I am. I work all day long to pay the bills and I want to be able to relax and do nothing when I come home."

Sara chose the word relationship. She defines her word as follows: "I want a man in my life who takes pride in his appearance. Someone whom I can take long walks with while having long meaningful conversations. A relationship to me is two people that always think of their partner and get closer and closer every day."

You can obviously see why this relationship is not going to work out. This is why the description of your word is so important.

Certainly, knowing each other's word will not alleviate all arguments, disagreements or mishaps. However, if any of the above begin, you at least know the core from which he or she is basing much of his or her reasoning. This may even help you to solve a misunderstanding before it becomes an argument.

Let me give you an example:

Teddi's word is <u>love</u> and Joey's word is <u>love</u>. To take it to the next level, we find out that <u>love</u> for Teddi means kindness to all. Listening and being there for people who need her.

While for Joey, "Love" means the campassion and attention of one woman. A woman who is always there for him.

Joey comes home one day and finds Teddi with her arms around Tom, a neighbor from next door. Teddi looks up and sees Joey and excuses herself from Tom.

If Joey didn't know that Teddi was all about being there for others and helping people, he might jump to conclusions about what he saw. But because he knows her, he patiently waits. She explains that Tom's father had passed away this morning. Then Joey goes over and puts an arm around Tom and consoles him as well.

Now if Teddi's word had been "Fun" meaning anything new and funky or "Experience" meaning trying new things or "Dangerous" meaning living on the edge, Joey probably wouldn't have waited for Teddi to come over.

Again this isn't to say that Joey's first thought wasn't to be upset. Perhaps, if Teddi hadn't seen Joey immediately and excused herself from Tom, there may have been an altercation.

Even if an altercation occurred, knowing Teddi's word and description of it would help Joey to realize she was being true to herself and remaining true to him.

It always helps to step back and think about something that has just happened. Having a word to think about and description of that word, will help to alleviate a lot of unnecessary frustration. Everyone would benefit by doing the same.

If Joey is frustrated with Teddi, Teddi also needs to look at Joey's word and what it means to him. Each person needs to respect the other's word.

Flexibility is very important too. There will be times that your word and the word of your partner may not seem to gel. Given that you both know your words and what they mean to each other, it should help you to meet in the middle, where there is understanding once again.

Some of the most difficult situations in life can be helped immeasurably, if there is love and understanding. If that does not exist, the words may stand on their own, each in its own slot, unwilling to change. Love mediates and brings people and their words closer together.

In summary, the only way to know if two words are compatible, is to take it to the next level. Find out what your partner's word means to him or her. There may be layers to explore in order to understand the depth of their commitment to their word. But it will definitely be worth the time to find out.

When you first approach your friend, partner or spouse, don't make finding their word a serious deal-breaker. Make this experience fun and challenging. Since you don't know their word, tread lightly when attempting to discover it.

Once it's out in the open, if you feel your relationship could move to the next level or you believe your relationship could be in trouble, you can ask more specific questions.

Share your concerns with your partner and ask them to share theirs. Never expect something from someone that you are not willing to do for them.

Once again, above all, do <u>not</u> judge your partner's choice of word. It is theirs and theirs alone. If you try to manipulate them into choosing a word that works for you, you are depriving yourself of the truth and making it harder for your partner to trust you.

This is about honesty and a willingness to learn about ourselves and the people we want to associate with.

Be open to learning about yourself and the other person.

Events that change your word?
(Death, near death, divorce, job loss, birth)

All the words listed above can definitely set a change in motion. All are traumatic and usually bring you to a place where you question things more readily and begin to re-evaluate your life and your purpose in it.

The most important thing to do before anything else, in the event of any of the occurrences listed above happening to you, is to sit for a while by yourself. Think about the word you chose or about choosing a word for the first time. It will give you purpose, which is what you will need desperately. Don't ask for help from anyone you know. Ask yourself or if you believe in a higher being, ask them. It's important that you take the time to do this. This will bring you to a place where it will help to make it easier to deal with the issues at hand.

Here are some examples of the emotions that may appear during these times:

If your word is <u>love</u> and you experience the death of a spouse, you may fear love and feel your word needs to change to something safer, where you won't be hurt. It is a misconception to believe, however, that had you chosen a different word, the outcome would be different. Your word is about you and not the person who has passed on. Your word was most likely right for the time being and may continue to be so, however, it may not seem that way for a while.

If you chose the word <u>Relationship</u> or <u>Comfort</u>, and you lose your spouse, you may feel abandoned and either become angry with the departed or angry with yourself for feeling as though you had reached your goal and wanted life to go on like that forever.

In this case, you may grow to need a different word that is not dependent on another, which frees you from the fear of loss.

If your word is <u>motherhood</u> or <u>fatherhood</u> and you lose a child, you may feel that God is punishing you for something, which of course is not the case. You will go over and over in your head what you must have done wrong to think your path was to be a mother or a father and have it taken away.

In this particular instance, you should go over and over in your mind, all the wonderful times you had with your child and be grateful for that. The words <u>Motherhood</u> and <u>Fatherhood</u> are powerful words and should not be diminished because the paths seem to have disappeared. You can choose another word that will allow you to find your strength again, but hold on to your original word as well.

The loss of a child for anyone is devastating, no matter what your word is, however if your word lives outside of <u>Motherhood</u> or <u>Fatherhood</u>, it is more likely that you can keep living with the thought of what your child would want you to do. It is a huge burden to bear either way.

A near-death experience will usually have you more available to a lot of possibilities. This would be an excellent time to choose a word or change your existing one.

Many times there is a clarity that comes with almost losing one's life. The closer you come to death, the more open you usually become afterward in learning you are still alive. You may begin a campaign to help others; make good on past debts; tell special people how you feel about them; and tell a story that you didn't know before this happened to you: the story of how precious life is. It is a profound and life altering experience, because it is you who have gone through it.

When others pass on, it is not freeing or wonderful. Although, people who have almost passed on, tell a story of beauty and freedom on the other side.

So this is definitely a time to choose a word that you cannot now imagine living without. It will probably be a very powerful word, indicative to your experience.

Divorce is another event that can definitely change the meaning of the word <u>Relationship</u> forever. However, this is not always a bad thing. There are many meanings for the word <u>Relationship</u> that are good and forwarding. You may need to only change the meaning and not the word itself.

Again, many individuals have chosen the word <u>Relationship</u>. However, the meaning of the word differs a great deal for each of them. Some see a relationship as something to fall back on, while others see a relationship as the piece that fulfills them. Still others see it as a union that makes them happy for the time being.

Your response to a divorce would depend heavily on the weight of this relationship through the explanation of your word.

And for many, of course, "Relationship" may not even be your word. The further your word is from attaching to another human being, the quicker you will be back on track with your own life.

It's wonderful to care for others and do what you can when you can. But you need to take care of <u>you</u> first.

You can't give what you don't have to begin with. And, if absolutely everything you are is invested in another individual and they leave, it will be a long and painful fall. It will feel as though half of you is missing and you can't go on.

But you can.

Choose a new word or renovate the old one. Then, direct your own path.

Losing your job is yet another earth-shaking occurrence that could definitely change the meaning of your word. In particular, if your word is <u>trust</u> or <u>success</u>, you may begin to question if your word really meant what you thought. You begin to wonder if it's truly what you want.

After you attain success in business and have managed to reside on this plateau for a while, the elimination of your job includes a steep fall, for which you are not usually prepared. The confidence you once had and the pride you felt begins to slip away. If you don't find another position to fill rather quickly, the need to change your word will begin.

Stay strong and always know that if you believe in yourself, others will too. It's not always about you. There are multiple factors involved in an elimination of a position that has nothing to do with you at all. This sounds absurd...considering you held the position, but it's true. And, you need to know this inside, so that you can go on with confidence.

This is actually a good time to sit down and think about the word you chose and why. What does it mean to you? Could it possibly mean the same thing to you, after losing your job? Could this be an opportunity in disguise? I think you can guess which thought would be the most forwarding.

Again, if you need to change your word, you can. However, don't do it from a place of anger or disappointment. Those things will pass, but if lingered on too long, will only hold you back. Do it from a place of forwarding empowerment. Once this is achieved, you can focus on your word and it will help you to see your path more clearly.

This is also a wonderful time to discover what your word is, if you haven't asked yourself this before. A new plateau; a different scenario; a new opportunity for growth. It's something you don't need anyone else's input to begin again on your life's path.

On a more positive note, the birth of a child definitely changes a lot of words. Many times, a woman hasn't taken on a word until she gives birth, then boom! It hits her and she knows her word is <u>Motherhood</u>. For a man whose word is <u>relationship</u> or <u>husband,</u> it can be troubling. There is more responsibility and sometimes he sees it as a gift with a negative factor. This child comes into the world and begins taking away love, time and money from him.

However, this can also be true for the man who thought having a baby would be wonderful, until it happens and he realizes the spontaneity he enjoyed with his wife has diminished due to extra responsibilities. For all couples, it's definitely a work-around to be sure, but for some individuals it becomes a much bigger task.

For the individuals who are overwhelmed with a birth of a child and not sure what to do... enjoy what is. Write your word down and see how it may connect to the birth of your child.

Here are some examples:

If your word is <u>passion</u> as in sports that you enjoyed every Sunday on TV, perhaps this could be a time to hold your new baby and explain the plays and scores. Whether it is a girl or a boy, you will provide a bond between the two of you and this child will probably grow to enjoy sports as well.

If your word is <u>appreciation</u> as in, you simply want people to notice the input you have put forth to bring about someone else's happiness, perhaps helping feed and change the baby will bring you and your spouse as well as you and your child closer together.

You may decide to change your word based on all of the instances discussed. However, you should take the time you need to decide if you truly want to change your word or you want to change the meaning of your word instead.

During a traumatic time, it's good to find a focus that can be forwarding. This would be a very good exercise to do to put you back on a healthy and forwarding path.

Something to always remember is that words become our reality. So when you are choosing your word, you need to realize that you are in command of your future and you are choosing the instrument that will guide you along the way.

It's the one thing that will always be up to you. Decide wisely.

Changing your word?

Once you've decided that you want to change your word, start from the beginning. In the situation you now find yourself in, list the words you feel fill your life.

Write down however many words it takes and then cut it in half. Do this until you are down to the one word that now Defines you. The one word that you feel you could not do without. Now write down the meaning of this word for you. This is your new word. Stay true to that word, but only for as long as it brings you what you're looking for.

It may be that you only need to give your original word a new meaning. However, you may also feel you've grown and are finding that what was important to you before is no longer important to you now. This is wonderful. Growth is always a good thing.

Changing your word can be a sign of moving forward, as long as it's not due to a suggestion made by someone else. It has to be something you alone own.

Meaning, if you are taking on a new word, because someone else feels they know you better than you know yourself and you accept that, I would think long and hard about your decision.

Choose your word and stand by it. If you are living your word, you will see how it affects others and whether or not this has you meet the goal you've given your word.

Secondary word?

There are always going to be a great many words that are associated with your word. So, there's no need to have a secondary one. However, if you feel extremely torn between your first word and a second, I would suggest writing down reasons why either word is right for you. I'm willing to bet that you will come up with one that exceeds the benefits of the other. But, if you are uncomfortable giving up the second word, keep it until you feel differently. Having a secondary word is definitely a personal choice.

But, most people will probably notice that if someone said they had to take away one of the two words, they would know which one to give back.

Don't forget, your word can hold the meaning of many words. As a reminder, you can return to the first chapter and read the words that I have in my life. Then see how I eliminated the ones I felt were also encompassed in the words I kept. I then narrowed it down to my one word, Love. And remember, every single one of those words will remain a part of my life. So don't be afraid to let some of your words go. They will remain with you, but not as the root of your essence.

Different Situations

Now that you've chosen: "What Word Defines You," here's how it can help you in the different situations listed below:

In a social context, you can make a game of it. While having fun, you'll find out, based on your word, who you might get along with and who you might not.

You'll find that for some, family is everything or being a mom is everything, while for others work is everything. Still for others it might be about finding happiness for themselves. So, you might like to know if the conversations you're in for are inundated with stories of poopy diapers, jelly smeared faces and a tower made from building blocks or if it will be a nonstop dissertation on the reasoning behind why paper that is .5 ounces as apposed .6 is much better for most laser printers and the black ink holds to the paper much better. Or you may run into someone who actually wants to know about you and your day and your likes and dislikes.

You'd be surprised to know how many people prefer one of the first two. You may not be comfortable talking about personal things or about yourself in general. You may enjoy having a discussion on the latest technology.

Again, depending on your word and explanation, it may or may not be something that would interest you. But, finding out ahead of time could remove a potential problem before it occurs.

In business, most people create friendships that are broadened to their personal lives. Given the fact that everyone spends a great deal of time at work, it would be nice to understand your new relationships a little better. A party outside of work may help.

In Hobbies, it mainly helps you individually. How many of us have sat there and thought, "I don't know what I like to do." However if you use your word and explanation as a base, you may be able to come up with something you never would have thought of otherwise.

Here's an example:

My word is <u>love</u> and I love being creative. So, when I was twenty years old, I rented an old theatre, produced and choreographed a Variety Special to benefit The Neediest Kids Fund and the following year, I did another for the Heart Association. This made a lot of sense to me because I got to use my skills and still stay true to the essence of who I am.

If your word is <u>adventure</u> because you love trying new things and meeting new people, you might think of joining an Explorer's Club or a group that does different things each month. You could pick and choose what it is you want to be a part of and see if it works.

In Community Activities, knowing your word may help you understand why certain activities don't do anything for you.

Here's an example:

You may have always said that you love being with people, but you find again and again that organizations you've joined do nothing for you.

It may be that your word is relationship and you unfortunately joined organizations that get together once a month to focus on completing a task that is mentally consuming. Therefore, no relationships are made.

Or, you joined an organization that is very harried and so there are no light and airy conversations or coffee time.

Knowing your actual word and explanation would help to explain why things do or don't work for you.

In Sports, you might need to see if you have a thick skin or not. It's usually a very competitive field. If your word is strength, challenge, growth, success or fun, it would probably be a good thing for you. However, if your word is love, me, faith or spiritual, maybe not. Not to say it's utterly impossible, but not as likely.

But as we discussed before, it depends what the description of your word is. It may not be at all how your word is perceived by others.

Conclusion

What's wonderful about finding your word and the description of it is that it's not only about intimate relationships or close relationships. It is a way to reach out and get to know more people. It will also help you to get to know why people feel, say or act the way that they do. It can really help us all to understand one another on a whole new level.

So start asking people you know today. What word Defines You? You'll get a puzzled look and you can laugh and say, "Do you wanna find out?" It's a great opening for a new friendship. You can start with your word and what it means to you. That usually relaxes people and they're more willing to participate.

By the way…

What *WORD* Defines You?

About the Author

Jeannie Brown has always believed that the knowledge we hold within ourselves is underestimated because the belief in ourselves is as well. All her life, she has done her best to be open to the knowledge and gifts that God and/or the world has given her, in order to help others do the same.

Writing has always been her favorite way of expressing herself. Another self-awareness book authored by Jeannie is "The Threshold," which she wrote because she believes in choice, possibility and the power of love. Changing genre's, her Conspiracy/Suspense/Romance series, "Deadly Desires" was published in 2017.

Jeannie produced, directed and performed in four theater productions to benefit charitable organizations. She received a plaque from the Heart Association for the Variety Special, "Vital Signs." Everywhere she works, she writes spiritual poems for birthdays, weddings. wakes and funerals.

The job title she seeks in life is that of a Loving, Caring Spirit. Her high spirit is known to her as Triacia-37, the essence of Love, which comes from her book, "The Threshold."

Love, integrity and truth are what guide her through life.

www.ingramcontent.com/pod-product-compliance
Lightning Source LLC
Chambersburg PA
CBHW072138280526
45788CB00002B/690

* 9 7 8 1 4 5 3 7 0 7 9 4 4 *